HOW TO READ A COMIC BOOK

Comic books are made up of pictures in boxes, called panels. Look at each of these panels from left to right, and top to bottom.

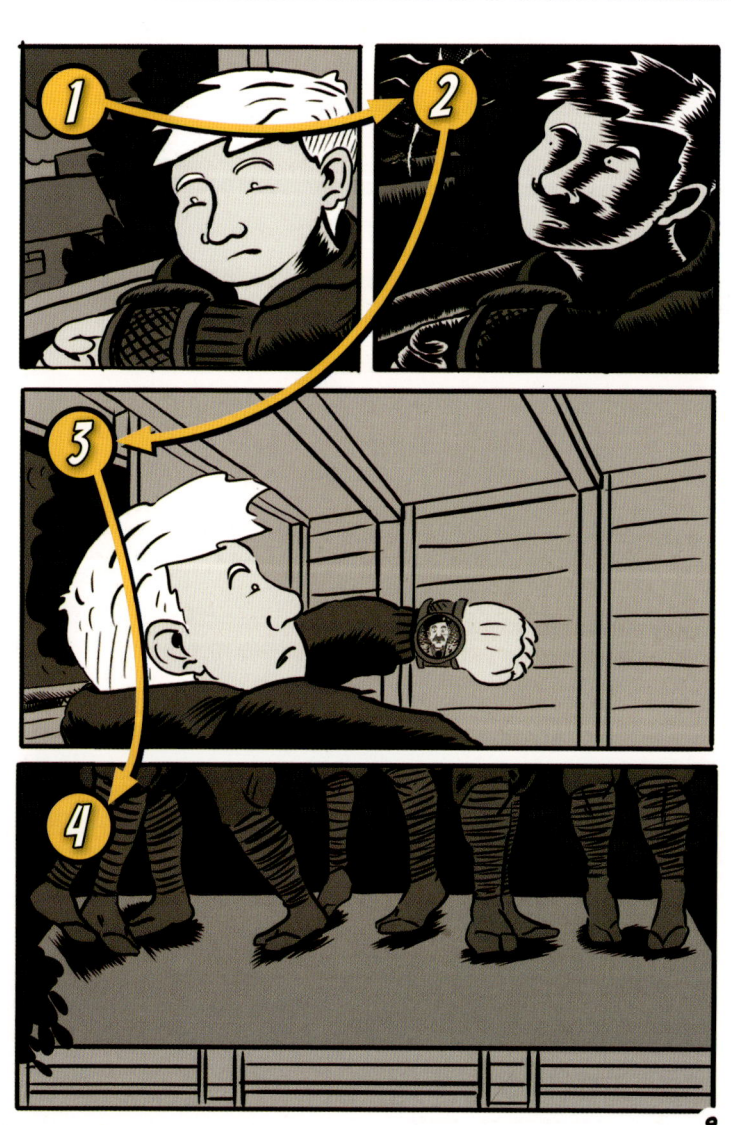

Read the speech bubbles, caption boxes and any sound effects from left to right, too. Together with the images, these will tell you the story.

IAN THE Bar-BEAR-ian

Written by
ROBIN TWIDDY

Illustrated by
WANQING WU

Oh dear.

ROAR!

I think he might be too stupid to die.

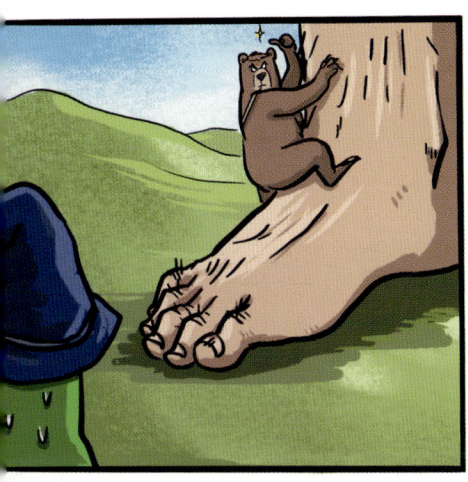

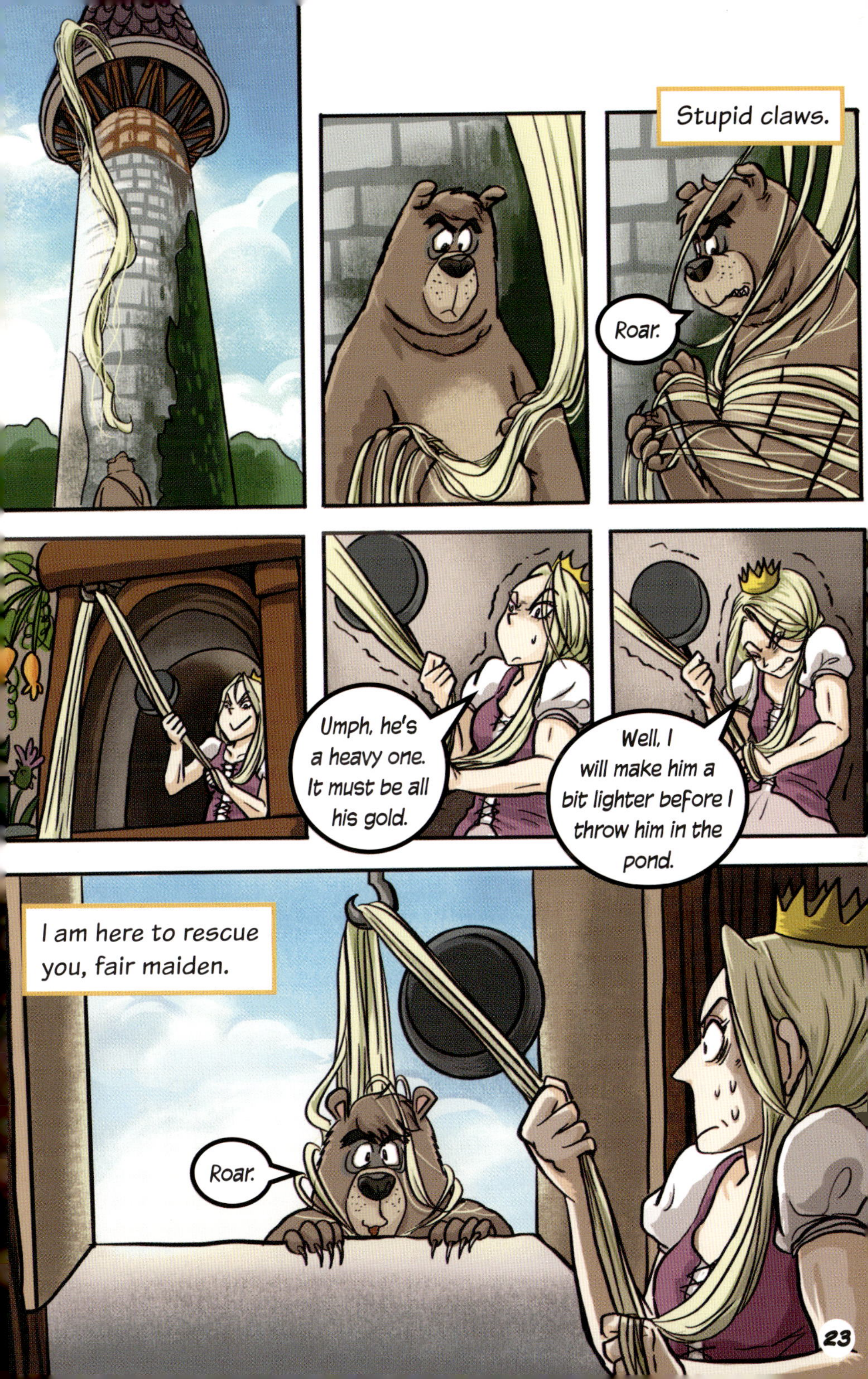

@2023 BookLife Publishing Ltd.
King's Lynn, Norfolk, PE30 4LS, UK

ISBN 978-1-80155-832-7

All rights reserved. Printed in China.
A catalogue record for this book is
available from the British Library.

Ian the Bar-BEAR-Ian
Written by Robin Twiddy
Illustrated by Wanqing Wu

ABOUT BOOKLIFE GRAPHIC READERS

BookLife Graphic Readers are designed to encourage reluctant readers to take the next step in their reading adventure. These books are a perfect accompaniment to the BookLife Readers phonics scheme and are designed to be read by children who have a good grasp on reading but are reluctant to pick up a full-prose book. Graphic Readers combine graphic and prose storytelling in a way that aids comprehension and presents a more accessible reading experience for reluctant readers and lovers of comic books.

ABOUT THE AUTHOR

Robin is a lifelong comic book fan whose love for the medium led to it being the topic of his undergraduate dissertation. He is the author of many great BookLife titles, including several entries into the BookLife phonic reader scheme. Robin loves action, adventure and humour, and brings these elements together into exciting narratives you won't forget.

ABOUT THE ILLUSTRATOR

Wanqing began drawing at a young age and never stopped. In the years that followed, she spent time working as a journalist. This experience provided her with an observant eye for detail and a thoughtful approach to her subjects. She carried these gifts over to her illustration work. It is through her art that she expresses this observant nature and her wonderful sense of humour. Her love for nature and wildlife almost led her to becoming a wildlife conservationist. However, now, Wanqing works as a freelance illustrator in London.